JUN 1 5 2016

D0606884

EXPLORING
CAREERS

Careers in Sales and Marketing

Barbara Sheen

ReferencePoint Press®

About the Author

Barbara Sheen is the author of eighty-nine books for young people. She lives in New Mexico with her family. In her spare time she likes to swim, walk, garden, and cook.

© 2016 ReferencePoint Press, Inc.
Printed in the United States

For more information, contact:
ReferencePoint Press, Inc.
PO Box 27779
San Diego, CA 92198
www.ReferencePointPress.com

ALL RIGHTS RESERVED.
No part of this work covered by the copyright hereon may be reproduced or used in any form or by any means—graphic, electronic, or mechanical, including photocopying, recording, taping, web distribution, or information storage retrieval systems—without the written permission of the publisher.

Picture Credits:
Maury Aaseng: 6
Thinkstock Images: 27, 35, 61

LIBRARY OF CONGRESS CATALOGING-IN-PUBLICATION DATA

Sheen, Barbara.
    Careers in sales and marketing / by Barbara Sheen.
        pages cm. -- (Exploring careers)
    Includes bibliographical references and index.
    ISBN 978-1-60152-812-4 (hardback) -- ISBN 1-60152-812-4 (hardback) 1. Selling--Vocational guidance--Juvenile literature. 2. Marketing--Vocational guidance--Juvenile literature. I. Title.
    HF5438.25.S4775   2016
    658.80023--dc23
                                                                                    2015009490

Contents

A Diverse Field

Approximately 250,000 new products and services are developed each year. Many of these items fail because they do not reach the right market, they are poorly advertised, or they are not sold by professionals who understand the business of selling. The job of marketing and sales professionals is to create and implement strategies to ensure the success of products before and during their life in the marketplace. As Jonathan Goldhill, chief executive officer and head marketing coach at the Goldhill Group explains in a March 13, 2013, article on Forbes.com,

> Think about how many products or services you have bought because of a compelling headline or guarantee, or because it requires an immediate response by you, or because you associated with the endorser or the testimonials from credible customers. Great marketing . . . promises performance or results. It compels you to like or favor a brand, a salesperson or influencer of the brand. And it drives you to desire a company's product or service.

Marketing and sales encompasses a large career field with diverse job activities. Although the duties and titles of marketing and sales professionals vary greatly, all these men and women have the same goal—connecting products and services with customers. Achieving this goal involves many different individuals focusing on a variety of tasks. For example, in order to offer the public the kinds of goods and services that will sell, marketing and sales professionals must understand how people make buying decisions.

Marketing professionals, known as market research analysts, focus on analyzing consumer surveys, sales data, and other statistics to make this determination. On the basis of these findings a team of other professionals, including product managers and product developers and designers, develop products and services to meet consumer needs. They also determine the price of these items based on the value customers give them. Other marketing professionals, such as channel sales managers and directors or managers of marketing and sales, use the findings to help set up distribution channels that best reach targeted customers. This might include placing items in specific retail stores, catalogs, and Internet sites where consumers who put the most value on the item shop. For example, marketers might place organic baby food in natural food stores and websites to gain the attention of those customers already interested in healthy eating.

In order to make the public aware of these goods and services and how they will enhance their lives, still other marketing professionals create and implement promotion campaigns. These individuals include a creative team of writers and artists who produce advertisements. The team also includes Internet and media specialists who develop a presence for the product or service on the Internet and in social media, as well as event planners and public relations specialists who plan promotional events geared to targeted customers. For instance, a toy manufacturer might promote an educational toy by exhibiting it at a teacher's convention.

Good marketing promotes sales. Sales involve the actual one-on-one selling of goods and services. This also encompasses a variety of jobs. Sales professionals work in both wholesale and retail sales. Retail sales personnel sell directly to consumers. They work in stores, on the phone as telemarketers, or out in the community as door-to-door sales representatives. Other sales professionals specialize in wholesale transactions. Rather than selling directly to consumers, these men and women deal with businesses, government agencies, hospitals, and other organizations.

A Place for Everyone

With such a range of job activities falling under the marketing and sales umbrella, there is a place for almost everyone. Careers in this field are perfect for individuals who like to be creative in solving

Sales and Marketing Occupations

Occupation	Entry-Level Education	2012 Median Pay
Advertising, Promotions, and Marketing Managers	Bachelor's degree	$115,750
Advertising Sales Agents	High school diploma or equivalent	$46,290
Cashiers	Less than high school	$18,970
Insurance Sales Agents	High school diploma or equivalent	$48,150
Market Research Analysts	Bachelor's degree	$60,300
Meeting, Convention, and Event Planners	Bachelor's degree	$45,810
Public Relations Specialists	Bachelor's degree	$54,170
Real Estate Brokers and Sales Agents	High school diploma or equivalent	$41,990
Retail Sales Workers	Less than high school	$21,410
Sales Engineers	Bachelor's degree	$91,830
Securities, Commodities, and Financial Services Sales Agents	Bachelor's degree	$71,720
Travel Agents	High school diploma or equivalent	$34,600
Wholesale and Manufacturing Sales Representatives	N/A	$57,870

Source: US Bureau of Labor Statistics, *Occupational Outlook Handbook*, January 8, 2014. www.bls.gov.

problems. It takes imagination to come up with the kinds of ads and promotional events that attract customers. Scientific minds are also needed. Some sales professionals, such as sales engineers, sell complex scientific and technical products to businesses. Since these men and women must be able to instruct customers in the use of these products, they must be knowledgeable about how these products work. And, since marketing and sales professionals must understand what compels consumers to make purchases, individuals interested in psychology and sociology feel at home in this career field, too.

Moreover, because marketing and sales are functions that are needed in practically every industry, individuals with a special area of interest can tailor their career in that direction. For instance, a person who is highly concerned about the environment can get involved in the marketing or sales of alternative energy equipment, while individuals who are passionate about cars or fashion can seek a marketing or sales positions in one of these industries.

Positives and Negatives

As with any career field, working in marketing and sales has both positive and negative aspects. Jobs in marketing and sales typically grow in proportion to the national economy. When the economy is strong, so is the marketing and sales industry. When it is weak, job growth slows. During the recession of 2007–2009 many companies cut positions in their marketing and sales departments. However, an improving economy, the increased intersection of technology with marketing and sales, and the expansion of international markets has helped improve job growth in the industry. Still, there can be a lot of competition for some marketing and sales positions. And these jobs are not as secure as they are in industries such as health care or law enforcement that are less tied to economic ups and downs.

Nevertheless, many marketing and sales professionals would not consider any other career. Jobs in marketing and sales are fast-paced, challenging, and exciting. No two days are ever the same. Industry personnel get to use their imaginations and interpersonal skills on a daily basis. They meet many different types of people and often develop long-term relationships with clients and customers. Extensive travel is common in certain jobs, and many marketing and sales executives have generous expense accounts, which they use to entertain clients.

There are also many opportunities for advancement and income growth. As California real estate agent Lisa Adams explains on the April 4, 2013, First Team Real Estate blog, "This career allows you to basically set your own destiny, that's what attracted me. The possibilities are endless. . . . I can't imagine myself doing anything else."

Advertising Account Executive

What Does an Advertising Account Executive Do?

An advertising account executive acts as a link between an advertising agency and its clients. He or she represents the agency yet attends to the wishes and concerns of the clients whose marketing interests he or she oversees. The goal is to ensure that the agency's work satisfies the client while earning the agency a profitable return for its efforts. An advertising account executive performs a myriad of job activities and works with many people in order to get this done. He or she handles every aspect of a client's account, from helping to plan an advertising campaign for the client to overseeing the campaign's production and launch.

This entails a number of steps. Before a campaign can be designed, the account executive meets with the client to discuss the product and the client's budget and business objectives. Next, the account executive confers with market research analysts who have been charged with evaluating the product's

---

At a Glance:
Advertising Account Executive

Minimum Educational Requirements
Bachelor's degree

Personal Qualities
Interpersonal skills; creativity

Certification and Licensing
None required

Working Conditions
Indoors, in an office

Salary Range
From about $37,000 to $124,000

Number of Jobs
As of 2015 about 170,000

Future Job Outlook
About average

sales potential and target markets. The account executive then prepares a report based on what he or she has learned from these sources and presents the report to the agency's creative team of artists and writers. Together they develop ideas for an advertising campaign that is customized to suit the client's budget and the target market.

The account executive also sets up a production schedule that establishes deadlines for different aspects of the project. As the project progresses, the account executive evaluates the work of the creative team, making sure that the advertising campaign clearly communicates the client's message and that deadlines are being met. He or she also coordinates with media buyers—professionals who purchase media space for the completed advertisement—and with Internet and social media specialists who create a public profile for the product on specifically chosen websites.

Throughout this process, the advertising account executive communicates frequently with the client, getting feedback on what the client thinks of the work so far. The account executive also holds follow-up meetings with everyone involved in the campaign, and he or she prepares reports for the client and for senior-level agency executives detailing the project's expenses, schedules, and progress. In addition to these job activities, the advertising account executive may also be responsible for bringing in new clients to the agency and maintaining existing accounts.

A May 5, 2014, article posted on the website of the Creative Group, a staffing agency that recruits talent for marketing and advertising firms, describes the job of an advertising account executive as "part stage manager, part juggler and 100 percent master of ceremonies. Today's advertising account executive knows how to keep clients happy while coaxing great campaigns from the creative team."

How Do You Become an Advertising Account Executive?

Education

To become an advertising account executive typically requires a bachelor's degree. Therefore, high school students interested in this career should take classes that prepare them for college. These classes should include English and speech to help develop students' oral and written communication skills. Advertising account executives use such skills in writing reports and in conferring with and giving presentations to clients and the advertising team. And, since these professionals work with numbers when dealing with budget matters, classes in math are also important.

In college, students can opt for diverse majors. Majors in marketing, advertising, or business are popular for this career. These majors offer classes in subjects such as consumer psychology, economics, market research, mass communication, and advertising media, which give candidates a good foundation and help them prepare for the different activities they will be expected to handle on the job. Classes in art, photography, and writing are useful, too. By giving future account executives an understanding of what goes into the work of the creative team, these classes can help candidates direct the progress of the agency's creative team in the future. Specific business writing and journalism classes help as well. They give candidates practice in creating clear, grammatically correct reports and other forms of written communication. And, because in planning an advertising campaign, advertising account executives must be able to assess consumer behavior, psychology classes are useful too.

Certification and Licensing

Advertising account executives are not required to have any license or certification.

Volunteer Work and Internships

Signing up for an internship at an advertising agency or in a company with an internal advertising staff is an excellent way to prepare for this career. Interns gain hands-on, real-world experience in advertising procedures. Under the supervision of an experienced account executive, they work closely with clients, the creative team, media specialists, and other advertising professionals. They may be involved in making creative decisions regarding advertising campaigns as well as preparing reports, presentations, and production schedules, among other duties. Competition for jobs in advertising is intense. In such a competitive field the connections interns make and the on-the-job training and experience they receive help them get jobs when they graduate. In fact, although most internships are unpaid, many interns go on to be hired by the firm for which they interned. As Melissa Benca, director of career services at Marymount College, explains in an April 14, 2010, article on CNN.com, "Internships have become key in today's economy. Graduating students with paid or unpaid internships on their résumé have a much better chance of landing a full-time position upon graduation."

College departments of advertising, business, and marketing help prospective advertising account executives find appropriate internship positions, as do organizations such as the American Association of Advertising Agencies (AAAA) and the American Advertising Federation (AAF). Indeed, becoming a member of a college chapter of the AAF is another good way to learn more about the industry and make professional connections. Student members are given the opportunity to attend guest-speaker events, participate in competitions, attend professional conferences, and network with other advertising students, professors, and industry professionals.

Skills and Personality

Account executives work with a wide range of people. They must be able to handle all types of people with tact and grace. Outgoing individuals with good people skills do well in this career. Excellent communication and leadership skills are also essential. Account executives chair meetings, give presentations, and write reports. They must be able to write and speak clearly to perform these duties effectively.

Moreover, in order to work with and direct the progress of the creative team, advertising account executives should be imaginative and have a sound understanding of the creative process. At the same time, they must be organized. Advertising account executives juggle many different duties. Coordinating multiple accounts, clients' requests, internal requests, advertising campaigns, scheduling, and budgets can be overwhelming if these duties are not handled in an orderly, methodical manner.

Other skills include being knowledgeable about market and social trends and consumer psychology. These factors are often the basis for a successful advertising campaign. Being comfortable using design, word processing, and budgeting software is also essential.

On the Job

Employers

Advertising account executives are employed by advertising agencies or large public and private firms that maintain an internal marketing or advertising department. Such firms can be found in almost every industry and range from companies that provide educational, health care, financial, or technical services to those that produce or sell consumer products. Most large advertising agencies are located in large cities, whereas companies with in-house advertising teams can be found throughout the United States.

Working Conditions

Advertising account executives work indoors, in an office environment. These professionals usually work full time for a minimum of forty hours per week. Many work more than forty hours per week in order to meet tight deadlines. They also may be required to meet with clients in the evenings or on weekends. Depending on the client's location, such meetings may involve travel to distant locations.

Account executives work with many people and teams of people on a daily basis. They often deal with difficult clients and coworkers. This aspect of the job, combined with strict deadlines, irregular work hours, and unexpected problems that often crop up make this a stressful career. In fact, the Business Insider website names a career as an advertising account executive as the sixth-most stressful white-collar job in the United States. To help ease the pressure, many companies offer relaxation lounges and well-stocked cafeterias to help employees unwind and refresh.

Earnings

Salaries for advertising account executives vary depending on the individual's level of experience, the geographic location of the business, and the type of business. Salaries range from about $37,000 to $124,000. The website Salary.com reports that as of 2015 the median salary for this career is $69,278. In addition to a base salary, account executives often receive large annual bonuses and profit sharing, which can significantly increase their annual income. However, such pay boosts are not guaranteed. Depending on the economy and the employer's profits, amounts can vary greatly from year to year. In some cases, advertising account executives are also paid a commission for the accounts they bring in.

Other perks include paid vacation and sick days, retirement benefits, and health insurance. Some companies also offer dental and vision care insurance as well as gym membership discounts to their employees. In addition, many advertising account executives have generous expense accounts that they use for travel and to entertain clients. Conducting business in a fine restaurant or at a major sports event is a common practice.

Opportunities for Advancement

Most advertising account executives start out as junior account executives. With about three years' successful experience they can advance to senior account executives. With continued success an individual can rise to the position of director of accounts services, who is the person that supervises and provides leadership for the entire accounts department. Moreover, because of their business expertise advertising account executives can also rise to management positions in almost any business setting.

Advertising account executives who earn advanced degrees may also opt to leave the business world to take a faculty position in departments of business, marketing, or advertising in colleges and universities.

What Is the Future Outlook for Advertising Account Executives?

The Bureau of Labor Statistics (BLS) estimates that employment for advertising account executives should grow about as fast as average from 2012 to 2022. However, growth in this industry is difficult to predict. Employment growth for account executives depends primarily on the economy.

Advertising budgets are usually tied to the economy. They are typically large when the economy thrives, which leads to job growth. When the economy is weak, advertising budgets usually contract. This decreases demand for employees. In addition, employment opportunities for these professionals are tied to the growth or lack of growth in the industries that employ them. Account executives will find fewer opportunities in declining industries such as the US steel industry, for example, and greater employment opportunities in flourishing high-tech industries.

Find Out More

Advertising Educational Foundation (AEF)
229 E. 42nd St., Suite 3300
New York, NY 10017
phone: (212) 986-8060
www.aef.com

The AEF is a nonprofit organization, supported by advertising agencies, whose mission is to help young people understand the role advertising plays in modern society. It offers information about careers in advertising and profiles of advertising professionals.

American Academy of Advertising (AAA)
e-mail: director@aaasite.org
website: www.aaasite.org

The AAA is an organization of advertising professionals, advertising scholars, and advertising students. It provides information about US colleges and universities that offer degrees in advertising. It also offers conferences, publications, and job lists for its members.

American Advertising Federation (AAF)
1101 Vermont Ave. NW, Suite 500
Washington, DC 20005-6306
phone: (800) 999-2231
e-mail: aaf@aaf.org
website: www.aaf.org

The AAF is an advertising trade organization. It represents advertising professionals and student members; offers information about internship opportunities in advertising; and sponsors college chapters, student competitions, and job fairs.

American Association of Advertising Agencies (AAAA)
405 Lexington Ave., 18th Floor
New York, NY 10174
phone: (212) 682-2500
website: www.aaaa.org

The AAAA is a national trade association of advertising agencies. It provides information about the advertising industry and sponsors a multicultural advertising intern program for qualified college students.

Director of
Marketing and Sales

What Does a Director of Marketing and Sales Do?

A director of marketing and sales is a high-level executive who manages a company's sales and marketing departments. His or her goal is to expand the company's growth by creating sales, marketing, and advertising programs that lead to increased profits and performance. This is a major task involving many different duties, which vary depending on the type and size of the company. However, certain job activities are shared by almost all marketing and sales directors. One of the most important is planning and setting his or her firm's annual marketing and sales objectives and coming up with strategies to attain these objectives. In order to do this, the director analyzes market research data, annual sales figures, and competitors' products, sales, and marketing activities. This information helps the

At a Glance:

Director of Marketing and Sales

Minimum Educational Requirements
Bachelor's degree

Personal Qualities
Leadership skills; good at multitasking

Certification and Licensing
None required

Working Conditions
Indoors in an office

Salary Range
From about $98,000 to $211,453

Number of Jobs
As of 2015 about 216,000

Future Job Outlook
About average

director to assess changing market and competitive conditions and come up with sales and marketing strategies that take these factors into account.

The director also takes into account the company's marketing and sales budget when planning marketing and sales programs. It is the director's job to create the budget and to ensure that what is spent on marketing falls within the designated budget. The director is also responsible for keeping track of marketing and sales performance. This involves preparing reports and presentations for other senior executives on marketing activities, sales volume, and potential sales.

In addition to these duties the director of marketing and sales serves as a team leader. It is this professional's job to manage the staff of the sales and marketing departments. Part of these duties includes recruiting, hiring, and training personnel as well as conducting performance evaluations. The director is also responsible for motivating the staff to increase productivity. In this capacity the director regularly meets with staff members individually and as a group to review the projects that each person is responsible for. He or she also establishes sales quotas and marks out sales territory for each sales representative, meets with sales representatives to brainstorm ways to increase sales, and sets up performance incentives and rewards. As Michaela S. (full name not given), director of sales at Yelp explains in a July 31, 2013, post on that company's website, "A typical day includes walking around the sales floors, talking and game planning with reps about pitches that they have lined up for the day. I meet with different managers, reps, and others within the company to talk about ways we can improve productivity and best practices for selling Yelp."

How Do You Become a Director of Marketing and Sales?

Education

Most marketing and sales directors have a bachelor's of business administration (BBA) degree. Many have a master's of business administration (MBA) degree. High school students interested in pursuing this career should take college preparatory classes. Courses in mathematics, which are needed to work with budgets and sales figures, are especially useful. Classes in language arts and speech improve a student's communication skills so that he or she can write and speak well. These skills are essential for writing reports and giving presentations. Many high schools offer business-related courses such as accounting, business law, and marketing. Electing these classes gives students a good introduction into subjects vital to their future career. In addition, since directors use different types of software in preparing budgets and reports, taking classes in computer technology is helpful too.

In college, many of these professionals majored in marketing. In general, marketing majors are required to take specific liberal arts classes such as English and speech as well as core business classes such as business statistics and economics. The latter introduce students to the world of business. Marketing classes are more specific to this career. In these classes students learn how businesses develop strategies for designing, pricing, distributing, and promoting goods and services. Specific courses delve into topics such as market research, marketing management, consumer psychology, international marketing, and promotion management, among other topics.

Certification and Licensing

No certification or license is required for a job as director of marketing and sales.

Volunteer Work and Internships

Prospective marketing and sales directors can learn more about this career and gain practical hands-on experience that will help prepare them for the future in a number of ways. One way is working in retail sales. This may be a part-time job or summer employment. Retail sales experience gives individuals an introduction to marketing strategies and consumer psychology and helps them develop interpersonal skills, such as tactfulness, which are needed to be a successful sales and marketing professional.

Another good way to learn more about a sales and marketing career is by joining a high school or college chapter of DECA. DECA is an association that encourages high school and college students to pursue careers in marketing. It provides its members opportunities to attend career development conferences and receive leadership training. It also sponsors a number of scholarships.

Doing an internship in marketing or sales is also very helpful. It gives marketing students the chance to convert the theoretical marketing knowledge that they learned in college into actual practice. Interns are usually given many responsibilities and receive ongoing training. They work side by side with experienced professionals, learning about marketing a product and the techniques used to secure a sale. Through hands-on experiences they gain valuable business skills that help them stand out from their peers. At the same time, they make professional and personal connections. These factors can help them gain full-time employment in the future. In fact, many employers say that the primary purpose of offering internships is to recruit new full-time employees.

Internships usually last at least three months, and some, especially sales internships, are paid. Most colleges help students secure internships. In addition, students can find internship opportunities by contacting specific companies they are interested in working for and by searching "marketing and sales internships" on the Internet.

Skills and Personality

First and foremost, marketing and sales directors must have proven expertise in marketing and sales. Most advance to this position after years of successful experience in other marketing and sales positions. This experience helps them to hone the skills they need to succeed as a high-level executive. Of these skills, one of the most important is having excellent interpersonal skills. Directors of marketing and sales work with many different kinds of people on a daily basis; establishing a good rapport with clients and coworkers is essential. Both clients and subordinates are more likely to be loyal to a person whom they like and trust. Being outgoing, friendly, and tactful go a long way in making this happen.

Good interpersonal skills also help directors be good leaders, as does having strong managerial abilities. These professionals must be able to get the best out of every member of their staff. Confidence, persuasiveness, and determination help directors to do so, as does respectfulness and tolerance of different types of people.

Being willing and able to delegate authority is part of this skill set, but these executives must also not be afraid to step up as the team leader and be accountable. Successful directors assume the weight of all decisions and take responsibility for all outcomes. At the same time, they stress that each member of their team should take pride in their work and hold themselves accountable for the work they do.

Two other aspects of being a good leader are having good judgment and being decisive. Directors deal with complex issues and make dozens of decisions every day. They must be capable of delivering quick, well thought-out solutions to multiple problems. Being critical thinkers who can draw correct conclusions based on market research data is an important part of making these decisions. So is using logic and reasoning to identify the strengths and weaknesses of different solutions to problems. Other important skills for this career include excellent communication and presentation skills, which are vital to writing reports, conducting meetings, and giving presentations. Knowledge of financial principles and mathematical skills are also necessary for analyzing statistics and preparing budgets.

On the Job

Employers

Some marketing and sales directors are employed by marketing firms that handle marketing for businesses that do not have an internal marketing department. However, most marketing and sales directors work for companies with in-house marketing and sales departments. These individuals may be employed by any sort of firm, from a charitable organization to a large multinational company.

Working Conditions

Sales and marketing directors work in an office environment. They typically have a private office and an assistant to help them with clerical duties. These executives typically work a standard forty-hour workweek, but they may be required to work longer hours during busy periods. In fact, working fifty hours a week is not uncommon. Additionally, sales and marketing directors are expected to attend promotional and networking events, trade shows, and seminars, which usually occur outside of office hours. Directors who work for companies that have branches in other cities may be required to travel to branch offices to conduct business.

This is a stressful job. Directors are under pressure to meet deadlines and performance goals. Many have sales quotas that their team must meet. Repeated failure to reach specified goals can result in job loss. Additionally, these professionals often receive or lose bonuses based on their team's performance, which can add to the stress.

Earnings

Directors of marketing and sales are usually well paid. Earnings vary significantly, depending on the industry, the company's size and location, and the director's education level and years of experience. The website Salary.com reports that as of January 2015 salaries for this career range from about $98,000 to $211,453 with a median annual salary of about $139,535. The Bureau of Labor Statistics (BLS) reports average mean salaries are highest in the following states: New York, $172,800; New Jersey, $156,670; Pennsylvania, $154,060; California, $153,180. It also reports that average mean salaries for this career are highest in the following industries: oil and gas; financial investment activities; nonmetal mining; and scientific research and development services.

In addition to their base salary, these professionals usually receive a generous employee benefits package that includes health insurance, retirement benefits, and paid vacations and sick leave. Directors of marketing and sales also receive performance bonuses that can considerably increase their annual income.

Opportunities for Advancement

Directors of marketing and sales already hold a high-level position in their career field. With an advanced degree and considerable successful experience as a director of marketing and sales, they can advance to company vice presidents, presidents, or chief executive officers. Some may opt to work as freelance marketing and sales consultants for multiple companies, which can be quite lucrative.

What Is the Future Outlook for Directors of Marketing and Sales?

According to the BLS, employment growth for this career is dependent on the growth or lack of growth in the industries that employ marketing and sales directors. With this in mind, it predicts that from 2012 to 2022, job growth for directors of marketing and sales is expected to increase about as fast as average for all occupations. There is strong competition for positions as marketing and sales directors, with many competent professionals vying for the best jobs.

Find Out More

American Marketing Association (AMA)
311 S. Wacker Dr., Suite 5800
Chicago, IL 60606-6629
phone: (800) 262-1150
website: www.ama.org

The AMA is one of the largest marketing organizations in the world. It provides information about marketing careers, publications, and webcasts. It also provides job listings.

Business Marketing Association (BMA)
708 Third Ave., 33rd Floor
New York, NY 10017
phone: (212) 697-5950
e-mail: info@marketing.org
website: www.marketing.org

The BMA is an association of marketing professionals, marketing students, and recent college graduates entering the marketing field. Its website offers job listings and a video on preparing an effective résumé. BMA also provides students and young professionals with career guidance and support.

DECA Inc.
1908 Association Dr.
Reston, VA 20191
phone: (703) 860-5000
e-mail: info@deca.org
website: www.deca.org

DECA is an organization made up of educators and high school and college students. It helps prepare students for careers in marketing and management. Members of the organization can attend workshops, enter competitions, and win scholarships. The website provides information about becoming a member.

Pi Sigma Epsilon
5217 S. 51st St.
Greenfield, WI 53220
phone: (414) 328-1952
e-mail: pse@pse.org
website: www.pse.org

Pi Sigma Epsilon is a coed national marketing and sales fraternity for college students and professional alumni with chapters in colleges throughout the United States. It sponsors conventions, competitions, leadership training, financial awards, scholarships, and website job postings for its members.

Internet Marketing Specialist

What Does an Internet Marketing Specialist Do?

The Internet plays a major role in modern life. Among other activities, people shop, manage their finances, conduct business, and communicate with their friends and family via the Internet. And, with the growing popularity of smart phones and tablet devices, individuals can access the Internet almost anywhere and stay connected twenty-four hours a day. As a consequence, the Internet has become an important way for companies throughout the world to reach consumers. Internet marketing specialists help companies to promote and sell their products and services online. Internet marketing specialists are also known as online marketing specialists, interactive designers, and digital marketing strategists.

Because this is a relatively new career field, the role of an Internet marketing specialist is not clearly defined. Conse-

At a Glance:

Internet Marketing Specialist

Minimum Educational Requirements
Bachelor's degree

Personal Qualities
Internet skills; writing skills

Certification and Licensing
None required

Working Conditions
Indoors, in an office

Salary Range
From about $37,000 to $95,000

Number of Jobs
As of 2015, figures not available

Future Job Outlook
Better than average

quently the responsibilities of the job vary among different employers. In general, these professionals are responsible for planning, implementing, and maintaining online marketing campaigns aimed at expanding a company's growth and profits. Their primary duty typically involves building up or revising the company's website so that it is an effective marketing tool. In this capacity the specialist considers a number of issues such as whether the website is user-friendly and attractive, whether it provides detailed product information, whether checking out and paying is fast and easy, and whether it is the type of tool that the target audience would utilize.

In order to identify their target audience and their online preferences and to track Internet trends and spot new marketing opportunities, Internet marketing specialists comb through databases, blogs, and competitors' websites. Then, with the help of the creative team, they use the information they have gathered to develop an online marketing campaign, which provides the target market with the type of content they prefer in a user-friendly format. Says Tania Rojas, senior product manager for Global E-Commerce at GoDaddy, "The most successful online stores know their customers' needs and sell them exactly what they want." Internet marketing specialists also measure and track the effect of their campaigns by using special web analytic software and spreadsheets.

One major concern is ensuring that the company's website is seen by as many people as possible. For this to happen it is essential that when shoppers search the Internet for a particular product, the website of the Internet specialist's company comes up in the search engine's top results. To boost the website's ranking on search engines, these experts use specialized computer programs that identify what keywords consumers are most likely to use when searching the Internet for their product. Then they make sure that these words figure prominently on the company's website, thereby improving their search engine ranking. This job function is known as search engine optimization. Some Internet marketing specialists focus only on search engine optimization. These individuals are known as search engine optimization specialists. Some companies employ both a general Internet marketing specialist and a search engine optimization specialist; some companies task the duties of both professionals to the Internet marketing specialist.

Internet marketing specialists are responsible for developing an online presence for businesses. This includes website development, tracking Internet trends, and planning, implementing, and maintaining online marketing campaigns.

Similarly, in many companies Internet marketing specialists are responsible for establishing, monitoring, and updating a social media presence for the company on sites such as Twitter, Facebook, Pinterest, LinkedIn, and Instagram; while in other companies a specialized Internet specialist, known as a social media specialist, handles this job. In either case, by providing frequent posts about the company on social media, the Internet marketing specialists help humanize the company. These posts include photos, videos, podcasts, and blogs. Moreover, by responding to consumers' posts, inquiries, and e-mails, the Internet media specialist helps to develop an interactive relationship between consumers and the business. These activities lead to increased sales. As marketing professional Suresh Babu explains on the Web Marketing Academy website, "When you're monitoring your customers constantly, their reviews, comments and conversations then it will be an easy task to come into the picture and help your customer when he needs you."

How Do You Become an Internet Marketing Specialist?

Education

This career typically requires a bachelor's degree. In preparation, high school students should pursue a college preparatory curriculum. In addition, they should take as many computer science classes as possible. Since Internet marketing specialists are charged with blogging and posting on social media, the ability to write well is vital. Language arts and creative writing classes help students to develop writing skills. Outside of school prospective Internet marketing specialists can hone their skills by studying different online marketing and social media sites.

In college, students should continue taking computer science classes. Specific classes in web programming, design, and development; computer graphics; search engine optimization; and blogging and social networking are essential. In fact, although it is not a requirement, many individuals enter this field with a degree in computer science. A major in a related field such as business, marketing, or communications is also applicable for this career.

Certification and Licensing

This career field does not require any certification or licenses.

Volunteer Work and Internships

Individuals interested in a career as an Internet marketing specialist must be tech savvy. Experimenting with web design, establishing a personal presence on social media, being active on various networking sites, and authoring a personal blog are good ways to build skills that will help in this occupation. In fact, if an individual has the skills to build up his or her own personal brand (the digital marketing term for a person's online persona) on social media, many employers consider this a good indication that the applicant has the ability to do the same for the company's brand. Consequently, many employers prefer such individuals.

Individuals can also add to their skill set by posting on a blog related to marketing or a personal hobby. Following the blogs of marketing industry experts is useful, too. It builds an individual's knowledge of his or her prospective career field. Volunteering to work on a political candidate's online campaign can also help build a prospective Internet marketing specialist's skills, as does taking a summer or part-time job in a marketing or advertising firm. In this capacity, individuals can learn about marketing and observe and interact with Internet specialists as they work. Doing an internship in these types of firms or in the marketing department of any company with an online presence further develops an individual's skills and offers practical on-the-job training and experience. It also helps individuals to network and make business connections. The connections and hands-on experience a person gains by doing an internship often lead to employment opportunities upon graduation.

Skills and Personality

Internet marketing specialists should have a strong knowledge of how the Internet works. Knowledge of HTML and at least one programming language such as Java Script or CSS helps these professionals in understanding website design possibilities and how users interact with online content. Along with technical skills, these professionals should have excellent writing skills. They are expected to create clear and interesting copy for blogs, social media, and websites. The more creative and innovative these are, the more likely they are to attract followers and new customers. Innovativeness and boldness are also needed to succeed in other aspects of this job. Digital marketing specialists are often the first professionals in a firm to try something that has never been done before. They must be able to take calculated risks based on the trends they identify in their research. Being analytical and persistent helps them to sift through data to identify such trends and understand the implications of these trends both on current and future marketing decisions. It also helps them in considering the relative costs and benefits of potential actions and to choose the most appropriate one.

In addition, these professionals must be able to work both independently and as part of a team. Good interpersonal skills help with the latter, and these communication skills are also important in responding to consumers' questions, comments, and complaints.

On the Job

Employers

Internet marketing specialists work for marketing and advertising agencies and for specialized digital marketing firms. They are also employed in almost every industry by large and small companies that have an in-house marketing division and an Internet presence. Some Internet marketing specialists are self-employed. These individuals act as independent consultants who offer their expertise to a variety of companies for a negotiated fee.

Working Conditions

Internet marketing specialists work indoors in an office setting. Those who work as independent consultants may work out of their homes as well as in the client's facilities. In either case, these professionals spend most of their time seated in front of a computer. This is typically a full-time occupation, although these specialists often work more than forty hours a week, especially when they are working on a large project. Moreover, since the Internet does not shut down at night, Internet specialists may be expected to monitor social media and the company's website at night and on weekends.

Earnings

Salaries for Internet marketing specialists vary widely. Earnings depend on the specialist's experience in the field as well as his or her training and education. The type and geographic location of the employer also impacts salaries. Generally, salaries are higher in private industry and in large cities where the cost of living is also high. According to Glassdoor, a website that helps match employers and employees and provides salary reports, as of 2015 salaries for Internet marketing specialists range from about $37,000 to $95,000. It reports the median annual salary for this occupation is about $56,816.

In addition to a base salary, Internet marketing specialists usually receive generous employee benefits. These usually include paid sick and vacation days, a retirement plan, and health insurance. In some cases vision, dental, and life insurance are also provided. Internet marketing consultants who are self-employed do not receive employee benefits.

Opportunities for Advancement

Individuals with successful outcomes as Internet marketing specialists can advance to digital marketing managers or directors. These are executives who supervise digital marketing teams. They may also advance to other managerial positions. With a strong track record, self-employed Internet marketing specialists can increase their fees and client base. They may be able to grow their business and hire other Internet marketing consultants to work for them.

What Is the Future Outlook for Internet Marketing Specialists?

Online shopping is predicted to grow significantly in the next few years. In fact, *Forbes* magazine reports that US online retail sales should reach $370 billion by 2017. Companies are increasing their spending and resources in this area in an effort to expand their Internet presence. As a consequence, jobs for Internet marketing specialists are expected to grow much faster than average.

Find Out More

Advertising Educational Foundation (AEF)
229 E. 42nd St., Suite 3300
New York, NY 10017
phone: (212) 986-8060
website: www.aef.com

The AEF is a nonprofit organization, supported by advertising agencies, whose mission is to help young people understand the role advertising plays in modern society. It offers information about careers in advertising, including interactive marketing careers. It also provides numerous informative links.

eMarketing Association (eMA)
40 Blue Ridge Dr.
Charlestown, RI 02813
phone: (800) 496-2950
website: www.emarketingassociation.com

The eMA is an international association of Internet marketers. It includes individuals, marketing students, and companies. The eMA offers networking opportunities, conferences, online classes, and a career center with job postings.

Internet Marketing Association (IMA)
10 Mar Del Rey
San Clemente, CA 92673
phone: (949) 443-9300
e-mail: info@imanetwork.org
website: http://imanetwork.org

The IMA is an international organization of Internet marketing, sales, and advertising professionals. It provides articles and news about Internet marketing, which can help prospective Internet marketing specialists increase their knowledge base.

Search Engine Land
website: http://searchengineland.com

Search Engine Land is a website that provides information about search engine optimization and Internet marketing. It provides news articles, blogs, networking opportunities, career information, and links to informative conferences.

Market Research Analyst

What Does a Market Research Analyst Do?

Consumers make many choices every day. It is the job of market research analysts to figure out what drives consumers to make the choices they do. Companies use this information to assess customer satisfaction and to determine what sort of products should be developed in the future.

In order to get answers, market research analysts spend hours collecting and analyzing facts and figures from consumer surveys, opinion polls, sales statistics, and other data. Then they prepare reports detailing their findings. One of the most important findings these reports describe is market demographics, or who the target market is for a particular product. Market demographics identify the age group, gender, income bracket, and other information about the people who are most likely to use a specific product. Companies use this information to determine how to promote the product, where to distribute it,

At a Glance:

Market Research Analyst

Minimum Educational Requirements
Bachelor's degree

Personal Qualities
Attention to detail; analytical skills

Certification and Licensing
Voluntary

Working Conditions
Indoors in an office

Salary Range
From about $33,460 to about $116,740

Number of Jobs
As of 2015 about 415,700

Future Job Outlook
Better than average

and how to price it. For example, if market researchers determine that the target market for a new item is teenage girls, the product is likely to be promoted on social media and teen magazines, endorsed by a celebrity that teenage girls relate to, and distributed to shops and Internet marketing sites that teens frequent.

Through their research, market research analysts also gather information about competitors' products and sales. This information includes what consumers say are these products' strengths and weaknesses and how they feel these products can be improved. This information is used in developing new products or modifying existing products so that their function, appearance, price, and other features best meet consumers' needs. For example, market research analysts working for a cell phone manufacturer might learn that customers want brighter-colored cell phones with larger screens. As a result, the company might change the design of its existing phone or develop a brighter, larger phone that suits consumer preferences.

Clearly the work of market research analysts has a huge influence on product development and marketing and sales strategies. As Stephen Griffiths says in a November 19, 2013, blog on the University of Wisconsin School of Business website,

> The work is fascinating. Whether celebrating the new iPhone 5 or watching a poor product disappear from the grocery store shelves, we have all wondered why we buy certain products and not others. . . . If you have ever wanted to design a new product, understand why people make buying decisions, influence advertising strategy, or change the layout of your favorite retailer, then marketing research could be the career for you.

How Do You Become a Market Research Analyst?

Education

Market research analysts are required to have a bachelor's degree. Many hold master's degrees. High school students interested in this

Gathering and analyzing sales statistics and the results of consumer surveys is a big part of the job of a market research analyst. The analyst helps companies determine what products to develop, who the likely buyers will be, and the best ways to promote and distribute those products.

career should take classes that prepare them for college. Classes in math and economics are especially important since market research analysts work with statistics and sales data. And, because these professionals must be able to work with spreadsheets, databases, and statistical software, computer science classes are also essential. In college, a major in business, economics, marketing, or statistics provides candidates with a good background for working in this career field. Classes in psychology are helpful, too. Besides collecting and analyzing data, market analysts use psychology to help them predict people's buying habits and what would attract a target audience to a product. Moreover, since these professionals must be able to clearly report their findings orally and in writing, classes in language arts and speech are vital.

Certification and Licensing

While market research analysts are not required to hold any certification or license, they can obtain voluntary certification from the Market

Research Association. This entails having at least three years' relevant work experience and successfully completing an exam. Being certified is prestigious and indicates a market researcher has demonstrated mastery of the profession. It can also help individuals advance in their career.

Volunteer Work and Internships

One of the best ways to learn about a market research career is by participating in an internship program. Serving as a market research intern gives candidates the chance to gain relevant work experience under the supervision of trained professionals. Interns often assist in conducting surveys, creating questionnaires, analyzing data, and preparing reports, among other duties. In many cases, upon graduation successful interns are hired by the company they interned with or by another firm, on the basis of experience, skills, and business connections they acquired on the job. Most colleges help students arrange internships in their chosen field. Depending on the particular internship, positions may be paid or unpaid.

In addition to working as an intern, other work or volunteer experience in jobs that involve analyzing data, taking surveys, or writing reports is also helpful. Becoming a member of DECA, an association that encourages high school and college students to pursue careers in marketing, is also useful. DECA members can attend career development conferences and leadership training events and network with the association's many business partners. DECA also sponsors a number of competitions and provides over $300,000 in scholarships.

Skills and Personality

Successful market research analysts are detail-oriented individuals. It takes a methodical person with intense focus and careful attention to detail to effectively sift through the large amount of facts and figures involved in precise data analysis. These professionals must also be comfortable working with numbers and be persistent and curious. Market research analysts spend most of their time problem solving. A large part of their job is determining the cause behind an occurrence, such as why sales of a particular product are declining. In many cases finding solutions can be difficult and time consuming. Market researchers who want to know why things happen and refuse to give up until they get answers are most likely to get the job done. Other character traits such as flexibility and open-mindedness also help market researchers to find solutions. Market research analysts must be flexible enough to employ multiple methods of acquiring data and different research strategies to solve problems. They also must be open-minded in coming up with solutions. Even if researchers have preconceived ideas about what the data will show, they must be objective in their analyses and able to adjust their thinking if the data proves them wrong.

Above all, these professionals should be analytical. They should be able to look at and break down data so that they can pinpoint patterns, trends, and problem areas. As blogger George Kuhn advised market researchers on April 21, 2012, on *The Research Bunker*, a market research blog for Research and Marketing Strategies (a Syracuse, New York, market research firm), "Don't look at the fact that 66% of customers have used the product in the past month. Look at what percent of those 66% are males/females, if they are females—What age are they? Do they have children? What type of job do they have? What is their income level?"

Good communication skills are also essential. Market research analysts write many reports and present information orally to marketing, advertising, and promotions managers. They, therefore, must be good writers and speakers. In addition to working with managers, these professionals often collaborate with other marketing professionals, including product developers, field interviewers who conduct surveys, and the advertising team. Therefore, they should be able to work as part of a team.

On the Job

Employers

Market research analysts are employed in almost every industry, including private businesses, government agencies, health care organizations, and colleges. Some work for private companies where they research market trends for the products and services produced by that company. Others work for marketing or consulting firms that do market research for many clients. About 5 percent of market research analysts are self-employed, serving as independent consultants. According to the Bureau of Labor Statistics (BLS), the management, scientific, and technical consulting services industry employs more market research analysts than any other industry, while the largest concentration of market research analysts, as opposed to other professions, are employed by the advertising and public relations industry. Market research analysts constitute 4.41 percent of all professionals employed by the advertising and public relations industry. Although these professionals can find employment throughout the United States, the BLS reports the following states employ the most market research analysts: California, New York, Texas, Pennsylvania, and Ohio.

Working Conditions

Market research analysts work indoors in offices. They spend a lot of time seated in front of a computer. These professionals typically work forty hours per week during regular business hours. However, they often work under pressure to meet tight deadlines, which may require overtime hours. It is not uncommon for market research analysts to work more than fifty hours per week at such times. Meeting deadlines can be stressful. In fact, *U.S. News & World Report* ranks stress levels for this occupation as above average. Market research analysts may be required to travel in order to meet with clients, attend conferences, or conduct research. The last may include working directly with the public collecting information through surveys, focus groups, and interviews.

Earnings

Salaries for this profession depend on experience, education, and the size, location, and type of employer. According to the BLS, as of May 2013 salaries for market research analysts ranged from about $33,460 to about $116,740. It reports a median annual salary of $61,290 for this occupation. It states that median annual salaries are highest for marketing researchers employed by the following industries: mining, semiconductor and electronic components manufacturing, motor vehicle manufacturing, and aerospace products and parts. It also reports the following states as having the highest median salaries for the profession: Washington, $78,580; Delaware, $77,620; California, $79,110; New Jersey, $75,750; Colorado, $77,970, and District of Colombia, $74,810. In addition to their base pay, most market research analysts receive employee benefits that include health insurance, paid vacation and sick leave, and retirement benefits. Those who are self-employed, however, do not receive a benefits package.

Opportunities for Advancement

Most market research analysts begin their career assisting experienced market research analysts. With experience, they are given their own research projects to tackle independently. Successful market research analysts may be promoted to market research managers, a position in which they supervise the market research division of a business or marketing firm. They may also rise to other management positions. In fact, many executives who work for corporations and government have a strong marketing background. Market research analysts with advanced degrees who want to teach often find positions at the post-secondary level.

What Is the Future Outlook for Market Research Analysts?

Market research analyst is one of the fastest-growing careers in the United States. One reason for this growth is that businesses are becoming increasingly aware of the importance of analyzing data for predicting consumer trends and ensuring growth. The BLS estimates that employment of market research analysts is expected to increase by 32 percent from 2012 to 2022. This is much faster than average for all occupations. The employment outlook is so bright for market research analysts in terms of job growth and salaries that in 2014 *U.S. News & World Report* named it the number one best business job and the fifteenth best job overall out of one hundred possible occupations in various career fields. Similarly, CNN Money named it the seventh best career out of one hundred occupations. Job growth is expected to be strongest in Seattle, Washington, and San Francisco and San Jose, California.

Find Out More

American Advertising Federation
1101 Vermont Ave. NW, Suite 500
Washington, DC 20005-6306
phone: (800) 999-2231
e-mail: aaf@aaf.org
website: www.aaf.org

The AAF is an advertising trade organization that represents advertising professionals and student members. It has college chapters and also offers information about scholarships and Internship opportunities in advertising and marketing and sponsors student competitions and job fairs.

American Marketing Association
311 S. Wacker Dr., Suite 5800
Chicago, IL 60606-6629
phone: (800) 262-1150
website: www.ama.org

The AMA is one of the largest marketing organizations in the world. It serves as a resource for marketers and provides job boards, information about marketing careers, publications, and webcasts.

The Council of American Survey Research Organizations (CASRO)
website: www.casro.org

This organization represents the market research industry. Its "Career Center" web page provides information about market research careers, including information about preparing a résumé appropriate for marketing jobs.

Marketing Research Association
110 National Dr.
Glastonbury, CT 06033-1212
phone: (860) 682-1000
e-mail: email@mra-net.org
website: www.marketingresearch.org
This is the largest professional organization of market research professionals. It holds conferences and training sessions, offers certification, and provides market research news, job listings, and information about a career in market research.

Product Manager

What Does a Product Manager Do?

Product managers are often referred to as mini chief executive officers. While they do not run companies, their role is to manage all the activities and functions related to a particular product from its conception and development to its marketing and sales. This entails performing a wide range of duties and working with many people. To start with, when a company comes up with an idea for a new product, the product manager is tasked with assessing the feasibility of the product. This involves investigating whether there is a need for the product and, if so, whether the product will expand the company's profits.

To gain information product managers use specialized analytic software to monitor market trends and market research data. This helps them to define the target market for the product, to gauge the target market's needs, and to evaluate competing products. Product managers also meet with market researchers and members of the company's finance and sales teams in order to get their input on these issues.

Once the product manager establishes that developing a particular product is a sound

At a Glance:
Product Manager

Minimum Educational Requirements
Bachelor's degree

Personal Qualities
Analytical abilities; creativity

Certification and Licensing
None

Working Conditions
Indoors in an office

Salary Range
From about $56,000 to $159,000

Number of Jobs
As of 2015 about 146,333

Future Job Outlook
About average

idea, he or she meets with design engineers and other professionals in the company's product development team. The product manager works with the team in designing the product, setting up a production schedule, and dealing with design and development questions and problems as they arise. As work progresses on the product, the product manager makes sure that the work is on track to meet the scheduled launch date. Although he or she does not have to be an engineer to perform this role, a product manager must thoroughly understand the product and what is involved in its creation in order to support the product development team and make informed decisions about the product. As Sebastian Cachia, product manager at Prezi, advises in a May 30, 2014, article on the All Things Product Management website, "If you are building software, then you should know a thing or two about programming, if your product tackles personal finance then you should know a thing or two about banking. This is not to say that you should try and do everybody's job, but make sure you are not the guy that always needs everything explained to them."

Before the product can be launched, the product manager has much more to do. These tasks include determining a pricing strategy for the product and planning and implementing a marketing campaign for it. Product managers analyze data and statistics and consult with the sales and finance teams in order to develop a pricing strategy. Similarly, product managers meet and collaborate with the advertising, marketing, and public relations teams to develop and implement a marketing campaign.

The product manager's job does not end once the product is launched. This professional is responsible for the product throughout its life cycle. This task is multifaceted, too. An important part is connecting with consumers in order to find out whether the product meets their expectations. The product manager gathers customer feedback by monitoring what customers have to say about the product on social media, running product testing groups, and analyzing market research data. When consumers report problems with the product, the product manager investigates the problems and, if applicable, works with the different teams to make changes to the product to better suit users' needs. At the same time, the product manager is charged with tracking the sales of the product. This involves analyzing sales data. If the product is not meeting business goals, the product manager once again meets with the development, marketing, and sales team in order to make changes either to the product or to the way it is being marketed in order to maximize profits.

How Do You Become a Product Manager?

Education

The minimum educational requirement for a product manager is a bachelor's degree. Many of these professionals have a master of business administration degree. In high school, students interested in this profession should follow a college preparatory curriculum. Mathematics classes are especially important. In fact, recruiters for product manager positions often look for individuals with experience working with numbers. This is because product managers collect and analyze lots of data and statistics. They use numbers to examine all aspects of profit and loss for their product. Therefore, successful product managers must be comfortable working with numbers. Computer science classes are also helpful, since product managers use a wide variety of software in their work.

In college, prospective product managers often earn a bachelor of business administration degree with a major in business administration, marketing, management, advertising, economics, or finance. Classes in communication and psychology are also important. Product managers regularly meet with a wide range of people. In order to get the best out of the various teams they collaborate with, product managers must be able to motivate and inspire others. In addition, product managers must be able to explain marketing concepts about the product to the design team, explain design concepts to the marketing and sales team, and so on. This requires good communication skills. In a November 2010 article on the Association of International Product Marketing and Management website, Laurie Jane, product manager director at Yesmail, explains, "One of the things I like about product management is communicating concepts to a variety of different audiences that may be new to the subject matter. In fact, there are some days when I feel more like a translator than anything else.

Not only do I attempt to translate or explain business initiatives to engineering and other stakeholders, but I also try and translate market trends and customer feedback into product ideas, product capabilities into positioning."

Certification and Licensing

Product managers are not required to have any special certificates or licenses.

Volunteer Work and Internships

One of the best ways individuals can learn about product management is by doing an internship in this field. This gives individuals an opportunity to use their existing talents and skills and hone new ones. Product management interns work directly with product managers. They are given real responsibilities, they attend team meetings, and they receive ongoing training. In many cases completing a successful internship is an excellent way for individuals to gain full-time employment upon graduation. Many firms present employment offers to the best interns, which they will fill after they graduate.

Individuals can learn about internship opportunities through their college or directly from companies at which they are interested in working. Most product manager internships are unpaid and occur during the summer months. This makes it possible for college students to gain work experience without delaying their studies. Internships are available throughout the United States, and many companies with overseas branches offer internships abroad to qualified individuals.

Skills and Personality

Since product managers perform diverse duties, a career as a product manager requires individuals to be versatile and have a wide skill set. For example, in order to effectively collect and use marketing research, these professionals should have strong skills in computer analysis, mathematics, statistics, data collection, and data interpretation. At the same time, these individuals are directly involved in creating advertising and marketing campaigns for their product, which requires creativity and imagination.

Product managers work with sales, marketing, advertising, finance, and the technical product development teams. In any given day they jump between meetings with different groups on different topics. They must be able to switch from one topic to another without losing track of the big picture. Since they are required to solve problems as they come up, these professionals need to be comfortable rearranging their daily schedule as needed. This requires that product managers be organized, flexible, and adept multitaskers. Additionally, to work efficiently with many different groups product managers need good leadership, interpersonal, communication, and listening skills. Indeed, the relationships that a product manager develops with the different teams helps drive the success of the product.

On the Job

Employers

Product managers have many possibilities in terms of employers. They work in almost every industry. To name just a few possibilities, product managers are employed by technology companies, the music industry, publishing, health care systems, the food and restaurant industry, and nonprofit organizations. Employers can be small start-up companies or large multinational firms. In fact, many large firms employ dozens of product managers.

Working Conditions

Product managers work indoors in an office environment. They often work in excess of a traditional full-time forty-hour work week, including working during evenings and weekends when necessary. Product managers may also be required to travel to meet with their clients. For example, product managers in health care–related companies often travel to hospitals where they observe the use of their products and talk to health care professionals and patients who use the products.

This job can be stressful. There is a great deal of pressure on these professionals due to numerous deadlines, schedule changes, and frequent meetings. Despite the stress, a 2010 survey conducted by Pay Scale.com and reported in the *Wall Street Journal* found that 52 percent of the product managers surveyed said they were happy or extremely happy with their jobs.

Earnings

Product managers are well compensated. Business Insider reports that the third highest ranked pay for workers at Google is that of product managers. According to the website Glassdoor, as of 2015 salaries for this profession ranged from about $56,000 to $159,000, with an average annual salary of about $111,650. Salaries are dependent on a product manager's training and experience and the location and type of employer. Generally, nonprofit organizations pay less than for-profit companies. Geographically, PayScale.com reports that the median income for product managers is highest in the following cities: San Jose, California; Dallas, Texas; Seattle, Washington; and Atlanta, Georgia.

Product managers usually receive compensation over their base salary in the form of bonuses and profit sharing. Depending on the company, these extras can add substantially to a product manager's wages. In addition, most product managers receive generous employee benefits, which include medical, dental, and vision insurance, retirement benefits, and paid vacation and sick days.

Opportunities for Advancement

Product manager is not an entry-level position. Most product managers begin their career as an assistant or associate product manager or in another aspect of marketing. Typically, assistant product managers need three to five years of successful experience before being eligible for a promotion to product manager. With successful performance, product managers can advance to become marketing managers, executives who are responsible for overseeing the company's marketing department. With their leadership skills and multiple areas of expertise, product managers can also advance to a position as a company's vice president, president, or chief executive officer. For example, Marissa Mayer, CEO of Yahoo, was once a product manager at Google.

What Is the Future Outlook for Product Managers?

The Bureau of Labor Statistics reports that all jobs in the field of marketing management are predicted to grow about as fast as average from 2012 to 2022. Employment growth, however, is dependent on the growth of the particular industry that employs a product manager. Employment opportunities, therefore, should be greater in expanding industries such as technology and health care than in less robust industries. The increasing globalization of marketing and sales should also increase job growth. Job opportunities are likely to increase for product managers with international marketing experience in companies that are marketing their products globally. In addition, many product managers are expected to reach retirement age within the next decade. As these individuals retire, their positions will need to be filled.

Find Out More

American Marketing Association (AMA)
311 S. Wacker Dr., Suite 5800
Chicago, IL 60606-6629
phone: (800) 262-1150
website: www.ama.org

The AMA is the largest marketing association in North America. It provides information about different marketing careers, including product management. It also provides job listings.

DECA Inc.
1908 Association Dr.
Reston, VA 20191
phone: (703) 860-5000
e-mail: info@deca.org
website: www.deca.org

DECA helps prepare students for careers in marketing and management. Members of the organization receive leadership training and can attend workshops, network with industry professionals, enter competitions, and win scholarships.

Product Development and Management Association (PDMA)
330 N. Wabash Ave., Suite 2000
Chicago, IL 60611
phone: (312) 321-5145
website: www.pdma.org

The PDMA is an international organization of professional product developers and managers. It offers job lists, information about graduate programs, and training.

Silicon Valley Product Manager Association (SVPMA)
300 Union Ave., # 26
Campbell, CA 95008
e-mail: pm_association@yahoo.com
website: http://svpma.org

The SVPMA is an organization of product managers. Its website provides links to many blogs and books about product management, which can help individuals learn more about this career.

Public Relations Specialist

What Does a Public Relations Specialist Do?

Public relations specialists help shape the public's opinion about an organization, business, or individual. Also known as press secretaries (when they are employed by government agencies or officials), media specialists, PR reps, or communication specialists, these professionals are tasked with generating positive publicity for their client and enhancing their client's public image. This is an important task because if the public has a negative impression of a product, service, individual, or organization, they are less likely to support or purchase it. As Mylene, a public relations manager for a nonprofit organization, explains in an interview on SchoolFinder.com, "I manage the public relations and marketing for the organization. This involves communicating and building relationships with people that we need to reach. These would include various stakeholders such as our members (our customers), influencers, industry/government representatives, educators, and the public-at-large."

At a Glance:
Public Relations Specialist

Minimum Educational Requirements
Bachelor's degree

Personal Qualities
Communication skills; interpersonal skills

Certification and Licensing
Voluntary

Working Conditions
Indoors in an office

Salary Range
From about $30,760 to $101,030

Number of Jobs
As of 2015, about 229,100

Future Job Outlook
About average

Public relations specialists have a number of duties. They serve as writers who create press releases, story pitches, presentations, and videos for the media about positive, newsworthy events concerning their client. For example, if a company sponsors a charitable event, the public relations specialist might write a press release for newspapers, magazines, radio, television, or a social media site detailing the company's role in supporting the charity. The goal is to make the public aware of how the company gives back to society, thereby raising the company's public image. Unlike in advertising, a public relations specialist's client does not pay the media for this coverage. Therefore, to ensure the news they want to share gets aired, public relations specialists work hard to establish and maintain good relationships with journalists, bloggers, and other media contacts. In fact, public relations specialists often act as spokespersons for their clients. In this role they talk to the media on their client's behalf. This often involves deflecting negative criticism. They might represent the organization they work for at community projects and conventions or by engaging directly with the media via phone, e-mail, or prepared press releases.

These professionals also work closely with top executives and important clients. They write speeches and set up speaking engagements, interviews, news conferences, and other forms of public contact for the company's top executives or important clients. To help the executives and clients prepare for such events, public relations specialists act as coaches. In this capacity they advise these executives and clients on public speaking and on their public image. Because speakers are judged not only by what they say but also how they say it, their body language, and their physical appearance, this coaching role is quite important.

To ensure that the speeches, presentations, and press releases they create will make a positive impact, public relations specialists do lots of research. This involves reading newspapers, magazines, and blogs in search of material pertaining to their clients. They maintain files of appropriate material, which they use to support their writing. They also use this information in internal publications such as company newsletters and stockholder's reports, which they are charged with writing and editing.

Writing and coaching are not the only way public relations specialists communicate with the public. They are responsible for developing and organizing special events that raise awareness about their company and enhances the company's image. Such events might include workshops, meetings, and public ceremonies. They may also be tasked with escorting visitors and clients.

How Do You Become a Public Relations Specialist?

Education

Most public relations specialists hold a bachelor's degree. Taking college preparatory classes helps high school students prepare for this career. Since public relations is all about communicating, classes in speech and language arts are especially helpful. Classes that help develop an individual's research skills are also useful.

In college, prospective public relations specialists often choose a major in a communications-related field. Majors in journalism, communications, public relations, or marketing are popular choices. Since public relations specialists help shape public opinion, courses in psychology and advertising are useful. Creative writing classes are also essential. Such classes help individuals hone their writing skills and become more confident writers. Similarly, classes in speech and theater help prospective public relations specialists become more skilled and confident public speakers.

Certification and Licensing

This occupation does not require any licenses or certification. However, public relations professionals can voluntarily acquire an Accredited in Public Relations (APR) designation through the Public Relations Society of America or an Accredited Business Communicator (ABC) designation from the International Association of Business Communicators (IABC). Holding either accreditation indicates competence in this field and may be useful in helping individuals advance in their career. To earn either accreditation, individuals must have a bachelor's degree and at least five years' experience in public relations, successfully complete an exam, and present samples of their work.

Volunteer Work and Internships

Young people can do a lot to learn about and prepare for this career field. Activities such as working on a school newspaper or yearbook, for example, are valuable experiences that help individuals learn how to write clearly and concisely. Promoting a school play, dance, club, or sports event is also a good way to practice some of the promotional and publicity skills that public relations specialists need. Running for a school office, too, is helpful. Candidates must write and give speeches. This can help individuals build the confidence, writing, and oratorical abilities that a job in public relations requires.

Taking a part-time or summer job in a public relations firm or in the public relations department of a large company is another great way to learn about this career and to gain some valuable work experience. Serving as a public relations intern is another valuable experience. Interns gain real-world public relations experience. They work with public relations professionals who guide, mentor, and supervise them, and they make industry connections. Gaining full-time employment in an entry-level public relations position is highly competitive. The experience and connections interns gain gives them an advantage over many of their peers.

Internship opportunities in public relations are abundant. Public relations firms, marketing and advertising firms, government, large and small companies, sports teams, publishing, and nonprofit organizations are just a few of the types of organizations that hire public relations interns. Most colleges help students find suitable internships.

Skills and Personality

Writing and speaking are key components of this occupation. Public relations specialists write speeches, press releases, and internal company newsletters, among other items, and they speak to the media, clients, top executives, and the public. To do their job well, they must have excellent written and oral communication skills. They should also be comfortable speaking in front of large groups; this takes confidence and poise. Speaking about the profession in an article on the website PR Crossing, public relations specialist Greg Day explains, "Communication is the key backed with energy and passion for what you are selling. There is some writing involved and plenty of meetings to attend, so you have to be organized, but it's performance as a communicator that counts."

Excellent interpersonal skills are also vital. In order to get the stories they want reported in the media, these professionals must establish good relationships with a wide range of people; being friendly, outgoing, and personable helps in forming and maintaining such relationships. Being persuasive and able to network effectively, too, help in this endeavor.

Public relations specialists should also be good problem solvers who can "think on their feet." When serving as a spokesperson for their client, they may be asked difficult questions. They must be able to state their views objectively and honestly without damaging their client's reputation. Sometimes, while serving as their client's representative, they may bear the brunt of criticism. They must be able to deal with such criticism gracefully without taking it personally. This takes a self-assured person with a thick skin.

On the Job

Employers

Public relations specialists are employed by anyone who wants to establish and maintain a strong public image. This includes large and small businesses, government agencies, nonprofit organizations, educational and health service organizations, and individuals such as sports figures, entertainers, and other celebrities. Many public relations specialists work for public relations consulting firms or advertising firms. The Bureau of Labor Statistics (BLS) reports the following industries as those with the highest levels of employment in this occupation: advertising, public relations, and related services; business, professional, labor, and political organizations; colleges and universities; and local governments.

Working Conditions

Public relations specialists work indoors in an office setting. They also give speeches, attend community activities and special events, and meet with clients outside the office. These activities may require travel. Public relations specialists typically work forty hours per week. However, they are often required to attend events on weekends and evenings. Moreover, should a situation arise in which the skills of a public relations specialist are needed, these professionals are expected to be available to deal with the situation without regard to the time frame.

Earnings

According to the BLS, as of 2012 public relations specialists earn from about $30,760 to $101,030 annually, with a median annual wage of about $54,170. Earnings vary depending on the type of employer, the location of the employer, and the public relations specialist's education and experience. The BLS reports the following states with the highest annual mean earnings for this profession: Virginia, $78,520; California, $71,390; Maryland, $68,290; and New Jersey, $67,430. In addition to their yearly salary, most public relations specialists receive employee benefits that include health insurance, retirement benefits, and paid sick and vacation days.

Opportunities for Advancement

As public relations specialists acquire experience, they advance in salary. With experience and proven capability, public relations specialists can be promoted to supervisory positions managing the public relations department of a large organization or as a manager in a public relations consulting firm. Some experienced public relations specialists start their own public relations consulting firms.

What Is the Future Outlook for Public Relations Specialists?

The BLS reports that between 2012 and 2022, opportunities for public relations specialists are predicted to grow by 12 percent, which is about as fast as average for all careers. This translates to approximately 27,400 new positions added to this career field. Additional job opportunities should result from the need to replace public relations specialists who retire or leave the occupation for other reasons.

Competition for entry-level public relations specialist positions is fierce. Many college graduates apply for the limited number of available public relations positions annually, and the number of qualified applicants is expected to exceed the number of jobs. Competition is predicted to be especially keen for entry-level public relations specialist jobs in advertising firms and at high-status public relations firms.

Find Out More

International Association of Business Communicators (IABC)
One Hallidie Plaza, Suite 600
San Francisco, CA 94102-2842
phone: (415) 544-4700
website: www.iabc.com

The IABC is an organization of communication professionals and students. It helps connect job seekers and employers and offers accreditation, workshops, conferences, and informative articles.

PR Council
32 E. Thirty-First St., 9th Floor South
New York, NY 10016
phone: (646) 588-0139
website: http://prfirms.org

The PR Council is a trade association of public relations firms. It provides career information, job postings, and interviews with young PR professionals who talk about their jobs.

Public Relations Society of America (PRSA)
33 Maiden Ln., 11th Floor
New York, NY 10038-5150
phone: (212) 460-1400
e-mail: prssa@prsa.org
website: www.prsa.org

The PRSA is the world's largest professional organization of public relations professionals. It offers student membership. It provides networking opportunities, salary surveys, job postings, and information about accreditation.

SchoolJournalism.org
American Society of News Editors, Youth Journalism Initiative
210 Reynolds Journalism Institute
Missouri School of Journalism
Columbia, MO 65211
phone: (573) 882-3792
website: www.schooljournalism.org

This website provides information about careers in journalism, including public relations; college journalism and communication programs; and scholarship opportunities. Its student advisory board is given opportunities to network and attend special events.

Retail Salesperson

What Does a Retail Salesperson Do?

Retail salespersons are also known as sales associates. Their job is to sell products directly to consumers. Such products include clothing, electronics, groceries, cosmetics, cars, furniture, and sporting goods, just to name a few.

Retail sales personnel work in all types of stores. They provide a number of services. One of the most important is helping customers find whatever they are looking for. This involves asking questions and listening to shoppers' needs. Once retail salespeople have gathered this information, they give customers advice and tell them about possible merchandise options that might meet their needs. When shoppers have specific questions about certain products, in order to best serve customers these sales professionals must be able to provide answers. For example, a retail associate who sells mattresses must know all the particulars about each mattress's features as well as the store's financing policy and warranty services. And, since increasing store sales is a retail sales associate's primary goal, once a customer decides on a product, sales

At a Glance:
Retail Salesperson

Minimum Educational Requirements
None

Personal Qualities
Interpersonal skills; persuasiveness

Certification and Licensing
None

Working Conditions
Indoors in retail stores; outdoors in car lots, lumberyards, garden centers

Salary Range
From about $16,830 to $38,820

Number of Jobs
As of 2015, about 4.7 million

Future Job Outlook
About average

associates are expected to provide customers with suggestions about purchasing other items that logically go with the original product. The mattress sales associate, for instance, might try to sell the customer pillows or a mattress cover, while a clothing sales associate might suggest matching accessories to complete an outfit.

Once a customer decides to make a purchase, the sales associate rings up the sale. Retail salespeople use cash registers to handle transactions. They are responsible for receiving cash, checks, and charge and debit card payments; making change; and keeping track of all the money inside the register. Sales associates also use cash registers to handle exchanges and merchandise returns. They are also responsible for packaging customers' purchases and arranging for deliveries. In some cases they gift wrap packages.

Sales associates have other duties, too. They are charged with housekeeping tasks such as ensuring that fitting rooms in department stores are ready for customers. This involves clearing out merchandise and returning it to the proper area of the selling floor. Similarly, they are responsible for maintaining selling floor presentations. In a garden center this might involve watering and deadheading plants, while in a clothing store it might entail folding and stacking shirts and sweaters. It also involves keeping counters and shelves neat and clean and in many cases preparing displays. These professionals are also responsible for restocking items. This means that if the selling floor is low on a particular product, the sales associate is responsible for bringing more of the product from the stockroom to the selling floor. Sales associates are also charged with taking inventory. This entails counting and recording the number of specific products in stock at a particular time.

How Do You Become a Retail Salesperson?

Education

This career has no minimal educational requirements. However, some retail businesses prefer that sales associates be high school graduates. Most businesses provide retail sales personnel with on-the-job training where they learn about customer service, cash register operation, and store policies. In addition, new hires in large stores usually work as a team with experienced sales associates who mentor them.

Taking certain classes in high school can help individuals prepare for this career field. For example, since sales associates handle money and take inventory, mathematics classes are useful; so are speech and language arts classes. These classes improve an individual's speaking and listening skills, which helps salespeople to communicate with customers effectively. They can also enhance an individual's ability to speak persuasively.

Certification and Licensing

Retail salespersons are not required to have any licenses or certificates.

Volunteer Work and Internships

Individuals can learn more about a career in retail sales in a number of ways. High school students can join DECA, an association of college and high school students interested in marketing, sales, and management careers. DECA offers young people many opportunities to learn about marketing and sales careers and to develop the skills needed for these careers. In many high schools DECA members operate the school store. This gives students a chance to see whether they enjoy retail work and to experience real-world business situations. In addition, most DECA chapters maintain an excellent relationship with the local business community, which can help members gain employment as a salesperson in the type of retail business they prefer. Club members also get to attend conferences, and participate in role-playing and decision-making events and competitions, all of which can help individuals acquire important work skills.

Participating in school or club fund-raising activities is another way young people can gain selling experience, as is working at a bazaar or a crafts fair. Still another way individuals can gain sales experience and learn about this career field is by taking a part-time or summer job in a retail store. Finally, following a retail sales associate as he or she goes through a workday is an additional way to learn more about this career path.

Skills and Personality

Retail sales associates should like working with and helping others. In retail sales, good customer service (the care a person receives before, during, and after a purchase) can make the difference between making and losing a sale. Good customer service also helps create customer loyalty, which results in repeat business. Individuals who are friendly, enthusiastic about the products they sell, and genuinely care about helping others are most likely to succeed in this profession. Indeed, whether it is fitting a bride into the dress of her dreams or selling a customer the tool he or she needs to fix a leaky faucet, retail sales personnel help others every day. In a September 19, 2014, article on the website Quartz, an electronics sales associate describes some of the ways he has helped customers and how important these experiences are to him: "I had to console weeping customers for a variety of reasons like, 'my husband just died and I don't know the password to his computer.' I helped a blind, older gentleman who was absolutely tickled with what an iPhone could do for him—read menus out loud using image recognition software. I'm eternally grateful for those experiences, and they've shaped who I've become."

Good communication skills are also essential to this profession. Sales personnel must be able to communicate effectively with customers, peers, and management, both in person and on the telephone. They also must be able to read and interpret documents such as delivery schedules, warranty information, and operating and maintenance manuals. Moreover, they must communicate using courtesy and tact. Retail shoppers often form an impression of a store by evaluating its salespeople. Therefore, retailers stress the importance of providing everyone with courteous service. This is not always easy. It is not uncommon for individuals having a bad day to take out their frustrations on salespeople. Sales personnel have to take the good with the bad. No matter what a customer says or does, sales associates are expected to be calm, polite, patient, and tactful. This requires self-control and emotional strength. It also requires empathy. Being able to look at a situation through the eyes of a customer is a valuable skill that can enable salespeople to provide customers with the highest level of service.

In addition to being emotionally strong, retail salespersons should be physically fit. Healthy, energetic individuals who prefer

A salesperson helps a customer choose jewelry. People who work in retail sales must enjoy talking and listening because they are often called upon to help customers make purchases ranging from jewelry, cosmetics, and clothing to electronics, cars, and furniture.

moving around to sitting behind a desk are best suited to this profession. Working in retail sales is physically demanding and fast paced, especially around holiday sales events. Sales associates are on their feet most of the day. The job involves a lot of walking, reaching, and grabbing. Depending on the type of store, retail sales associates may also have to stoop, kneel, crouch, climb ladders, and lift heavy items.

On the Job

Employers

Retail salespeople are employed by large and small stores that sell all types of merchandise. Those who own their own stores are self-employed. Salespeople can opt to work in or own a store that sells products that they are passionate about. For example, someone who loves fashion can work in a clothing store, while a musician can work in a music store. This allows individuals to be surrounded by things they love and to share their expertise with others.

Working Conditions

Most retail salespeople work indoors in clean, well-lit stores, although some may work outdoors even in bad weather. The latter includes sales personnel in car dealerships, garden centers, and lumberyards. All retail sales personnel stand on their feet for extended periods of time, and, depending on the store, sales associates may have to get permission from a manager to leave the sales floor for any reason.

Retail sales personnel usually have flexible hours. According to the Bureau of Labor Statistics (BLS), one-third of all salespersons work part time. Because stores try to accommodate shoppers' schedules, work hours for both full-time and part-time sales personnel typically include evenings and weekends. Salespersons are often expected to work overtime during peak sales periods and are frequently required to work on holidays. They also may be required to work irregular hours. For instance, sales associates in some retail establishments are required to start work at midnight on Black Friday, a peak sales day that begins the winter holiday shopping season.

Earnings

The BLS reports that retail salespersons earn from about $16,830 to about $38,820 per year, with an annual median income of $21,010. Although most salespeople are paid an hourly wage, some retail salespeople are paid a commission in addition to, or instead of, a salary. This means that they are paid a predetermined percentage of any sales that they make. Being paid a commission has its advantages and disadvantages. Good salespeople can earn far more money than they would on a fixed salary, but the amount a person earns is not secure. This can be a problem during economic downturns when sales decrease.

In addition to their earnings, most retail salespersons get generous employee discounts on store merchandise. In some, but not all, cases sales personnel receive employee benefits that include health insurance, retirement benefits, and paid vacation and sick days. Salespeople who own their own stores do not receive employee benefits.

Opportunities for Advancement

As retail salespersons gain experience, they are given opportunities for advancement. They can move to managerial positions in which they supervise other retail sales workers. Those who work in large stores can move to a department of their choice. This allows workers on commission to move to positions selling higher priced items, which offer higher earning potential. Some experienced salespersons opt to open their own stores. These may be small businesses in which the owner is the sole salesperson, or they may be larger shops with more personnel.

What Is the Future Outlook for Retail Salespersons?

The BLS reports that between 2012 and 2022, the employment rate for retail sales workers is expected to grow about as fast as average for all occupations. However, according to the BLS, job growth for retail sales personnel in large superstores and warehouse stores is expected to grow much faster than average. This is because these businesses are expected to see strong business growth in the next few years. It should be noted that, in general, employment opportunities in retail sales grow when the economy flourishes and decrease during economic downturns.

Find Out More

AOL Jobs, "Ten Best Retailers to Work For"
website: http://jobs.aol.com/articles/2011/11/17/10-best-retailers-to-work -for

Based on the response of retail workers, this article lists the ten companies retail salespersons say are the best to work for, including the pros and cons of each company.

DECA Inc.
1908 Association Dr.
Reston, VA 20191
(703) 860-5000
e-mail: info@deca.org
website: www.deca.org

DECA helps prepare students for careers in marketing and sales. Members receive leadership training and can attend workshops, network with industry professionals, enter competitions, and win scholarships.

Education Portal
website: http://education-portal.com

The Education Portal website provides information about various careers. The article "Retail Sales Associate Career Information," describes what the job entails, how to become a retail sales associate, earnings information, and alternate career options.

National Retail Federation (NRF)
1101 New York Ave. NW
Washington, DC 20005
phone: (800) 673-4692
website: https://nrf.com

The NRF is the world's largest retail trade organization, representing retailers throughout the world. It offers numerous articles about the retail industry, information about a career in retail sales, job postings, and provides scholarships for students and retail workers who want to continue their education.

Sales Representative

Sales representatives, or sales reps, as they are also known, sell all types of products directly from manufacturers or wholesalers to businesses, government agencies, and other organizations. Any company that produces a product can hire a sales representative to represent them. Most sales reps specialize in selling within a particular industry such as medical supplies, engineering components, or consumer goods. Typically they are assigned a region or territory and take care of customers' needs within that region.

Selling a product takes a lot of effort. First, sales reps must identify and contact prospective customers by telephone, e-mail, or in person. Whenever it is possible, sales reps use "leads" to identify prospective customers. Leads are people or companies who have expressed an interest in the product. This group includes former and existing customers. Sales reps also make "cold calls." This involves making unsolicited calls to strangers in an attempt to sell goods or services.

Once contact is established, sales reps schedule meetings with prospective buyers. During these meetings sales reps assess the client's needs and provide them with solutions that fill

At a Glance:

Sales Representative

Minimum Educational Requirements
High school graduate

Personal Qualities
Interpersonal skills; self-confidence

Certification and Licensing
Voluntary

Working Conditions
Indoors with frequent travel

Salary Range
From about $37, 270 to $147, 320

Number of Jobs
As of 2015, about 1.9 million

Future Job Outlook
About average

these needs. As part of this process sales reps educate the client about the product they are selling. This entails giving a preplanned presentation that the sales rep has developed just for this purpose. The sales representative must also be prepared to answer any questions the prospective customer has about product. Therefore, sales reps must know a great deal about the specific industry and products they represent. In a 2009 article on the website Inside Career Info, a pharmaceutical sales rep explains, "Some folks are really interested in the technical aspects and the biology behind how the drugs work in the body; others just want to know what the expected end result is. So you really have to know the bottom line and the details behind it."

If the client is interested in purchasing the product, sales representatives are usually empowered to negotiate the price. Once a price is agreed upon, the sales rep takes the client's order. The sales rep fills out forms, enters orders into a computerized system, and schedules deliveries. Sales reps must maintain detailed records of their sales. They are also tasked with keeping records of their sales visits, maintaining customer lists, and filing expense reports.

A sales representative job is not over once a sale is made. By providing clients with ongoing customer service, sales reps cultivate relationships with their clients, which is a key to repeat sales. As part of this service they stay in touch with clients and help them with any problems that may arise concerning the product. They make sure deliveries are made as scheduled and that clients are satisfied with their orders. In many cases, once clients receive delivery of the product, sales representatives provide training to the clients and their staffs on how to best use the product.

How Do You Become a Sales Representative?

Education

Educational requirements for sales representatives vary according to the industry and the area of specialization. In general, a high school diploma is required for sales representatives in nonscientific and nontechnical fields. Sales representatives in technical and scientific sales need a bachelor's degree. These positions include, but are not limited to, sales representatives of pharmaceutical goods, medical supplies, and industrial equipment. In fact, many industrial equipment sales representatives have a bachelor's degree in engineering. Similarly, medical supplies and pharmaceutical sales representatives are likely to have a degree in biology or chemistry, and some are former health care professionals.

High school students interested in becoming a sales representative can take various routes to prepare for this career. Those interested in pursuing a scientific or technical sales career should take classes in subjects related to their chosen career field, such as biology, chemistry, and physics. These classes prepare them for higher-level college courses in these subjects.

Other classes are useful for all prospective sales reps no matter their specialty field. For example, speech and language arts classes improve an individual's speaking and listening skills. These skills are essential to communicating with clients and to giving effective presentations and training sessions. Since sales reps use computers to fill out forms, record data, and send e-mail, computer science classes are also useful.

Prospective sales representatives who attend college usually major in a field that is related to the industry in which they hope to work. For instance, courses in mechanical engineering prepare individuals interested in selling industrial equipment, while courses in computer science prepare individuals interested in selling computer software. Other classes in marketing and psychology are also important. Marketing courses give students an understanding of the various aspects of the selling process, while psychology courses help individuals understand the human mind and what motivates customers.

Certification and Licensing

No specific license or certificate is required for sales representatives. Some sales representatives voluntarily obtain a certified sales professional (CSP) credential or a certified professional manufacturer's representative (CPMR) credential. These credentials identify individuals as experts in their field and may help them advance in their careers. To obtain these credentials, candidates must have at least two years of successful experience as a sales representative, complete a formal sales training program, and successfully complete a written and oral exam.

Volunteer Work and Internships

Having previous sales experience can help individuals gain full-time employment as a sales representative. It also gives them the opportunity to test whether they like selling. Such positions range from selling items to neighbors as part of a fund-raising event to working in a retail store.

Doing an internship is another good way to learn about this career field while gaining on-the-job experience. Sales representative interns work under the direct supervision of experienced professionals. They are typically given opportunities to perform tasks such as identifying prospective clients, preparing deliveries, and tracking customer sales information. These activities help them to develop some of the skills that a professional sales representative needs to succeed. Internships in this field may be paid or unpaid. In some cases, interns earn a commission.

Skills and Personality

Sales representatives should be outgoing, assertive, and persistent. These personality traits help them to acquire clients and make sales. It takes confidence and assertiveness to make cold calls to strangers and to give presentations. And, since not every call leads to a sale, sales representatives cannot be discouraged easily. To succeed they must be persistent. Moreover, since an important part of making repeat sales is building relationships with clients, sales representatives should have good communication and interpersonal skills.

Being cordial and tactful and having self-control is essential. Sales reps have to deal with a variety of situations in a businesslike manner. For example, a sales rep may have an appointment with a client only to find that the client is not in his or her workplace at the scheduled time. Although the sales representative may feel frustrated or angry, he or she must handle the situation calmly and professionally. Moreover, a successful sales rep is flexible. Whether a situation involves changing his or her schedule to meet a client's needs or altering a presentation that is not working, the sales rep should be able to adapt quickly whenever change is needed.

Determination, motivation, and drive are other essential traits that sales representatives should possess. Sales reps are expected to meet or exceed sales goals determined by their employers within a targeted time frame. They must have the determination and drive to work toward these goals. In addition, since many sales representative positions are commission-based, the most successful reps are highly motivated individuals who are willing to do whatever it takes to make a sale. As an industrial safety products sales representative explains on the Inside Career Info website, "To work in my position, you need to be motivated. . . . You must be determined to get through to some companies to introduce them to and eventually sell them safety supplies. . . . It can be hard getting through the first few calls."

Moreover, in many companies sales reps compete against each other. Those individuals whose sales bring in the most money are rewarded with promotions, cash bonuses, and prizes. Not surprisingly, competitive individuals do well in this occupation.

On the Job

Employers

Sales representatives work in almost every industry for a variety of employers. They may be employed as in-house sales reps. These individuals are employed by a business to sell the products that it produces. Other sales reps are employed by a sales agency. Sales agencies do not buy the products they are selling. Instead, they operate on a fee or commission basis in representing the product's manufacturer. Still other sales representatives are self-employed. These independent sales reps contract with different companies to sell their products in exchange for a commission.

Working Conditions

Most sales representatives work in an office environment. Some work from home. However, sales reps spend a great deal of their time traveling to and visiting with clients. They are usually assigned a sales territory, which can encompass a small area, or it can cover several states. If the latter is the case, sales reps may be away from home for several days or weeks at a time. Most sales representatives work full time. Typically, they call on clients during regular business hours. Self-employed sales representatives set their own hours.

This can be a stressful career. Sales representatives are under a lot of pressure to meet sales goals. Not doing so can result in sales reps losing their jobs. The pressure to sell is even greater for those who depend on commissions for their earnings.

Earnings

Sales representatives' annual earnings vary according to the type of firm, the location of the firm, and the product sold. Most employers use a combination of salary and commissions or salary plus bonuses in determining a sales rep's salary. Independent sales representatives usually are paid only commissions. Commissions are generally based on the value of sales. The Bureau of Labor Statistics (BLS) reports that as of 2012 salaries range from about $37,270 to $147,320. It reports the following industries with the highest paying mean annual salary for this occupation: computer and peripheral equipment manufacturing, $113,440; oil and gas extraction, $105,080; apparel wholesalers, $98,650; and wholesale electronics, $98,370.

In-house sales representatives and those who work for a sales agency usually receive employee benefits that include health insurance, paid sick and vacation days, and retirement benefits. They also usually receive expense reimbursement related to business travel and entertaining clients. Independent sales representatives do not receive employee benefits or expense reimbursements.

Opportunities for Advancement

Sales representatives who consistently meet and exceed sales goals are most likely to be promoted. Promotions may entail being assigned a larger sales territory or a territory with greater sales potential. Successful sales reps may also advance to a management position with a title such as territory or regional sales manager, or director of sales.

Regional sales managers set sales goals for a specific region and supervise the sales representatives assigned to that region. Directors of sales oversee the entire sales team employed by the company.

What Is the Future Outlook for Sales Representatives?

Job growth for sales representatives is predicted to grow as fast as average for the period from 2012 to 2022, according to the BLS. Employment growth is predicted to be greatest for sales representatives working for sales agencies, since many companies are increasingly using these organizations as a way to cut costs in lieu of hiring in-house sales representatives.

Find Out More

AIM/R
800 Roosevelt Rd., Suite C-312
Glen Ellyn, IL 60137
phone: (630) 942-6581
e-mail: info@aimr.net
website: www.aimr.net

This association of independent manufacturing sales representatives connects independent sales reps with employers. It has a video on its website that offers insights into the role of independent sales reps.

Education Portal
website: http://education-portal.com

This website provides information on different careers. An article on the site titled "Pharmaceutical Sales Career Information and Education Requirements" offers information about becoming a pharmaceutical sales representative and includes a video about that career.

National Association of Sales Professionals
555 Friendly St.
Bloomfield Hills, MI 48341
website: www.nasp.com

This association of sales professionals provides job listings, résumé tips, and numerous informative articles about sales careers. It also offers certification and online training toward certification.

U.S. News & World Report
website: http://money.usnews.com

In an online article titled "Best Business Jobs Sales Representative" *U.S. News & World Report* provides an overview of the sales representative career, including information about training and salary, advice from people working as sales representatives, and job listings.

Interview with a Retail Salesperson

Larry Rulmyr is a retail salesperson at Mountain Music in Las Cruces, New Mexico. The store, which Rulmyr owns, specializes in the sale of new and used musical instruments. He has worked as a retail salesperson for thirty-five years. He spoke with the author about his career.

Q: Why did you become a retail salesperson?

A: I love music and instruments. Years ago, I ran a PX [a commissary on an army base] in Germany. It gave me a sense of retail sales and how to run a business. When I returned to the United States, I formed a band and went on the road playing music. But the idea of opening a music store was a pipedream I had. So, when I got a little money, I opened a very small shop and I've kept doing it ever since.

Q: Can you describe a typical workday?

A: As the only salesperson in the store, I do everything. Before the store opens, the first thing I do is get cash for the register drawer. Then I batch credit card receipts from the day before. [Batching is the process of taking the credit card transactions from the previous day and sending them to a processing bank. It is not until batching takes place that the card is actually charged.] Next, I make phone calls. There might be someone I have to call to let them know if we sold an instrument if it was on consignment, or I make follow-up calls to customers or people selling used instruments through the store. Once we open, it's sales throughout the day. That involves being here, waiting for customers to come in, and helping them to find exactly what they are looking for. I try to give personalized customer service. I know most of my customers' names and what type of equipment they like. I give out suckers to kids when parents bring them into the store.

Then, there are all the other things I do when I'm not waiting on people. A big part of retail is finding things to occupy your time when customers are not in the store. One thing I do is accept guitar shipment deliveries. I sign for the packages, unpack, inspect, and price the guitars. Then I put them on the sales floor. I also try to keep the store clean. I wipe down the showcases with glass cleaner and I clean the floors, so the store looks nice. I spray with air freshener and open the doors, so it smells fresh. Another thing I do is keep a list of the number of customers and sales for each month. I make a little graph of this information. This allows me to know how things are progressing. I also spend time reviewing trade catalogs and planning for future instrument orders.

Q: What do you like most and least about your job?

A: I like the satisfaction of doing well in sales and getting people the instruments that I know they are going to enjoy. I wake up each morning and I can't wait to get to the store. I love being around instruments and musical equipment. I also like the people that I deal with. If I were to retire, I would probably miss the people the most.

Back to the people, what I like least are argumentative customers. Although they are few and far between, there are some argumentative people who come in and argue about the price of an instrument. There's a lot of competition with big box stores, catalogs, and internet stores. Lots of small stores go out of business. Some people walk into the store checking their phones for prices and you are negotiating and negotiating. As a small business owner and salesperson, I hope people will support a local business, even if they have to pay a little more.

Q: What personal qualities do you find most valuable for this type of work?

A: Being nice, respectful, and businesslike. It does not cost you anything to be nice to people. I think if you're nice and respectful to everyone that walks in the door without judging them because of their appearance, you will succeed in retail sales. You have to be respectful. You can't get mad at people. You don't yell and scream. You must be calm and businesslike all the time.

Q: What advice do you have for students who might be interested in this career?
A: Simply have a passion for whatever you want to do. Enjoy what you do, take pride in doing a good job, and be honest with your customers. Being honest has kept me around for thirty-five years.

Other Jobs in Marketing and Sales

Advertising Media Coordinator
Art Director
Cashier
Catalog Sales Fulfillment
    Manager
Channel Marketing Specialist
College Instructor
Copywriter
Customer Service
    Representative
Database Marketing Manager
Demographer
Graphic Designer
Illustrator
International Marketing
    Executive
Insurance Agent
Marketing and
    Communications Manager

Meetings, Conventions, and
    Events Planner
Model
Online Community Manager
Packaging Specialist
Photographer
Photo Stylist
Product Development Manager
Purchasing Agent
Real Estate Agent
Retail Buyer
Sales Engineer
Securities, Commodities, and
    Financial Services Sales
    Agent
Telemarketer
User Interface Artist
Web Designer

Editor's Note: The US Department of Labor's Bureau of Labor Statistic provides information about hundreds of occupations. The agency's *Occupational Outlook Handbook* describes what these jobs entail, the work environment, education and skill requirements, pay, future outlook, and more. The *Occupational Outlook Handbook* may be accessed online at www.bls.gov/ooh/.

Index